Walking to Good Purpose
The Parish Churches of Exmoor
by *Tony Chapman*

ISBN 0 9535321 0 0

A CIP catalogue record for this book is obtainable from the
British Library.

Printed by West Somerset Free Press, 5 Long Street,
Williton, Taunton, Somerset TA4 4QN.

Published by the author

Index to starting places

1	Challacombe (Barton Town)	5
2	Kentisbury Church	12
3	Hillsford Bridge, Lynton	17
4	Lynmouth	22
5	South Molton (*Central Car Park*)	28
6	Exford	35
7	Exford	41
8	Porlock (*Central Car Park*)	45
9	Wheddon Cross	53
10	Dulverton	62
11	Dulverton	70
12	Wimbleball Lake (*Car Park*)	75
13	Dunster	81
14	Treborough	88

Index of Churches

	Walk Number	Page
Brendon	4	27
Brompton Regis	12	79
Challacombe (Barton Town)	1	8
Churchtown (Luxborough)	9	59
Countisbury	3	20
Culbone	8	52
Cutcombe	9	58
Dulverton	10	67
Dunster	13	85
Elworthy	14	96
Exford	6	38
Exton	10	68
Hawkridge	11	73
Kentisbury	2	15
Leighland	14	93
Luccombe	8	50
Lynton	3	21
Martinhoe	1	11
Molland	5	34
Monksilver	14	95
Nettlecombe	14	94
Oare	4	26
Parracombe (Christchurch)	1	9
Parracombe (St. Petrocks)	1	10
Porlock	8	49
Roadwater	13	87
Selworthy	8	51
Simonsbath	6	40
Stoke Pero	7	44
Timberscombe	9	60
Treborough	14	92
Trentishoe	2	16
Twitchen	5	33
West Anstey	11	74
Winsford	10	69
Withiel Florey	12	80
Withycombe	13	86
Withypool	6	39
Wootton Courtenay	9	61

Grid References of Starting Places   Walks

Barton Town, Challacombe	680406	1
Dulverton	912279	10
Dunster	992437	13
Exford	855384	6 & 7
Hillsford Bridge	740478	4
Kentisbury	622438	2
Lynmouth	724494	3
Porlock	885468	8
Treborough	011364	14
Wimbleball	967309	12
Wheddon Cross	925388	9

WALKING TO GOOD PURPOSE
THE PARISH CHURCHES
OF EXMOOR

Introduction:

Exmoor is one of our smallest National Parks. While it may be overshadowed in some respects by the greater size and grandeur of nearby Dartmoor with all those magnificent Tors and remoteness, Exmoor has a uniqueness and quiet beauty all its own. A fifteen-mile walk will provide a wide variety of landscapes and views ranging from lush wooded valleys to wild untamed moorland with breathtaking coastal scenery. Some of its villages and hamlets are a joy to behold. This guide is not the result of some grand premeditated plan but rather, like Topsy, "it just grew". Over the years I have come to love Exmoor and endeavour to spend as much time as possible walking over it and I also happen to be receptive to the restful atmosphere of our old churches and churchyards. Thus it seemed a good idea to plan a series of walks which would take in every Parish Church within the National Park Boundary, with a photograph of each and which would give a focal point to my outings for a few weeks at least. Having started out on the programme and become enthusiastic about it the obvious question came to mind, "Why not make it the subject of a guide?" After all, many Dartmoor walkers "collect" post boxes, so why should Exmoor walkers not collect churches?

The walks vary in distance from 10 miles to 18 miles with an average of 15 and are designed to provide as much variation in scenery as possible with enough geographical lumps to make the average walker feel he/she has had a good day's exercise. Of course there is nothing to stop the enthusiasts from extending the individual walks as they please. All the walks are circular on the assumption that most people will operate with just one car and in no case have they been arranged with convenient pub or cafe facilities being available. In some cases such places do lie on the route, but it has been assumed that the average walker will carry the necessary victuals for the day in the rucksack. Anyone proposing to do these walks will naturally have all the right equipment which includes, good boots, warm and waterproof clothing.

Although Exmoor is small and there is little possibility of becoming irretrievably lost it is always advisable to carry a compass and, for lone walkers, a whistle. After all, the fittest among us can trip or otherwise find ourselves incapacitated. When walking alone I always leave details of the day's programme and an estimated time of return. These are elementary precautions which amount to no more than common sense, which will be familiar to all serious walkers.

Some thought has been given to the question of maps. At first, the idea of line drawings of the routes was considered but quickly abandoned as experience suggests they are inconvenient on a number of counts. The walker will spend too much time with eyes glued to the directions lest the slightest navigational error renders him lost. If determined concentration maintains the walker on the straight and narrow then most of the delightful views will go unnoticed and distant features will of course remain unidentifiable. Any slight diversion is very difficult to correct if nothing more than a line drawing is to hand.

The OS have produced a 2 1/2" to the mile map covering Exmoor on one huge double-sided sheet, OUTDOOR LEISURE MAP 9 - EXMOOR. This is the one to use in spite of a big disadvantage, namely the sheer size of the thing which is approximately 3 x 3 feet. Handling such a large map on the top of Exmoor with half a gale blowing in off the sea and rain sweeping across horizontally is a fascinating, if infuriating experience. 'For those with ingenuity it might be possible of course to cut a sapling out

2

of the hedge, lash the map to it and thereby be sail-assisted (if the wind is blowing in the right direction). The old 2½" PATHFINDER SERIES were much smaller and far more convenient but unfortunately are no longer being produced, so we are obliged to use the Leisure Map. It is possible to purchase Waterproofed versions but these are expensive to buy. What can be done is to cut the map into two pieces vertically down the middle, peg each section on the washing line, spray with a proprietary waterproofing liquid obtainable from sports shops and leave to dry thoroughly. One last point on the subject of maps. It is a great help to go over the proposed route with a highlight pen. This will not obscure the detail but make it much easier to read and thereby allow the walker to enjoy the surroundings much more fully.

The starting places for the individual walks have been chosen with a view to safe parking for the car. This does impose some limitations on choice but it does seem sensible to leave the vehicle in a place where it will still be intact at the end of the walk. Worry about the safety of the car will spoil the pleasure of a good day out on the moor. In the case of Kentisbury and Barton Town (Challacombe) the car will be left outside the church and a farm since there are no alternatives and in both cases it is helpful as well as good mannered to call at the farm to ascertain the most convenient place to leave it. Where a number of walks use the same starting point (e.g. Exford) the local church will be referred to in the first walk from that place.

All the churches on Exmoor are very old and in the majority of cases have a rich and interesting history. In planning to do these walks time should be allowed for a good look both inside and outside these treasures. Time so spent will be most rewarding. One of the sad things is the realisation that so many of them are in urgent need of repairs and restoration and with so few parishioners in these scattered areas, funds are desperately needed from visitors. Another unfortunate development is the decision in one or two cases to keep the churches locked owing to the activities of thieves and thugs which although not entirely unexpected nowadays is a sad commentary on the times. Since precision is not essential in an exercise of this sort the walks include two churches, namely Molland and W. Anstey which strictly speaking are not on Exmoor. However they both lie very close to the southern boundary and each has all the characteristics of the area so it is hoped that purists will accept this minor departure from exactitude.

Readers should note that reference to Exmoor in this guide refers to that part which is included within the National Park boundaries and not necessarily to the wider area generally called "Exmoor".

Many of the churches referred to have now produced splendid little leaflets describing them in some detail which visitors will find very interesting. A number also have postcards showing photographs of the churches which will be a useful supplement to any the walkers may take.

Tony Chapman   1st May 1997

Cover Illustration.
Oare Church

© **Tony Chapman**
September 1998

Walk No. 1: BARTON TOWN (CHALLACOMBE) - YELLAND CROSS - PARRACOMBE - FOLLY CORNER - MARTINHOE - MANNACOTT LANE HEAD - HUNTERS INN- KILLINGTON - EAST MIDDLETON - ROWLEY CROSS - BROCKENBARROW - BARTON TOWN.

14/15 miles. A fairly gentle day's walking.

Churches: Challacombe - Parracombe (2) Martinhoe.

Commence at Barton Town. First of all call at the farm to ascertain the best place to park. The farmer is helpful and appreciates motorists with the manners to ask. Begin by walking up Barton Lane to Yelland Cross and carry on northward along the path opposite which leaves Whitefield Barton on the right. Follow this path all the way to Parracombe bypass and having crossed over it continue into Parracombe turning left to Christchurch, main church of the village.

After looking around this impressive old place, follow the road round to St. Petrock's Church to the east. Continue from this church along the footpath bounding the old Heddon House which comes out on to the old road through Parracombe. Turn right here to Parracombe Lane Head and Killington Cross.

Proceed with care along the main A39 for a short distance where a footpath leaves the road and crosses fields, finally arriving at Folly Corner. From Folly Corner the path across fields leads directly into Martinhoe, another delightful and, happily, unspoilt Exmoor hamlet overlooking the sea. After enjoying the beauty of Martinhoe and filling the lungs with bracing (sometimes very bracing) sea air it is time to look round and start the trip home.

Continue on the road used to enter Martinhoe and into Berry's Ground lane to its end at Mannacott Lane Head at which junction turn right past Mannacott Farm and along King's Lane.

Summoning up all the power of abstemious rectitude pass the old and very enticing Hunters Inn and without an overdose of regret turn south to pass Milltown, Tucking Mill and Mill Farm. This lovely walk along the River Heddon ends just past Mill Farm, where the road bears left and carries on past Kittitoe and Killington. Less than half a mile up the hill from Killington House there is a footpath to the right (if you reach Killington Cross you have gone a short distance too far). Follow the sign to Higher Bodley which continues straight on to where the surfaced road ends and keep on this path until a 'T' junction is reached. Ignore the left turn into Bodley and instead turn right and carry on to Skilly Cottages, West Hill Farm and to the county road. On reaching the road turn left passing Higher East Middleton Farm and turning right at Minniemoor Cross to Rowley Cross. Leave the road here and follow the signed footpath to Brockenbarrow some mile or so to the south. This path reaches to B3358 just below Brockenbarrow Farm at which point there is a somewhat uncomfortable half mile walk along the road to Yelland Cross. Turning into Barton Lane will bring relief from the mad motorists and another half a mile brings us back to the starting-off point.

Walk 1

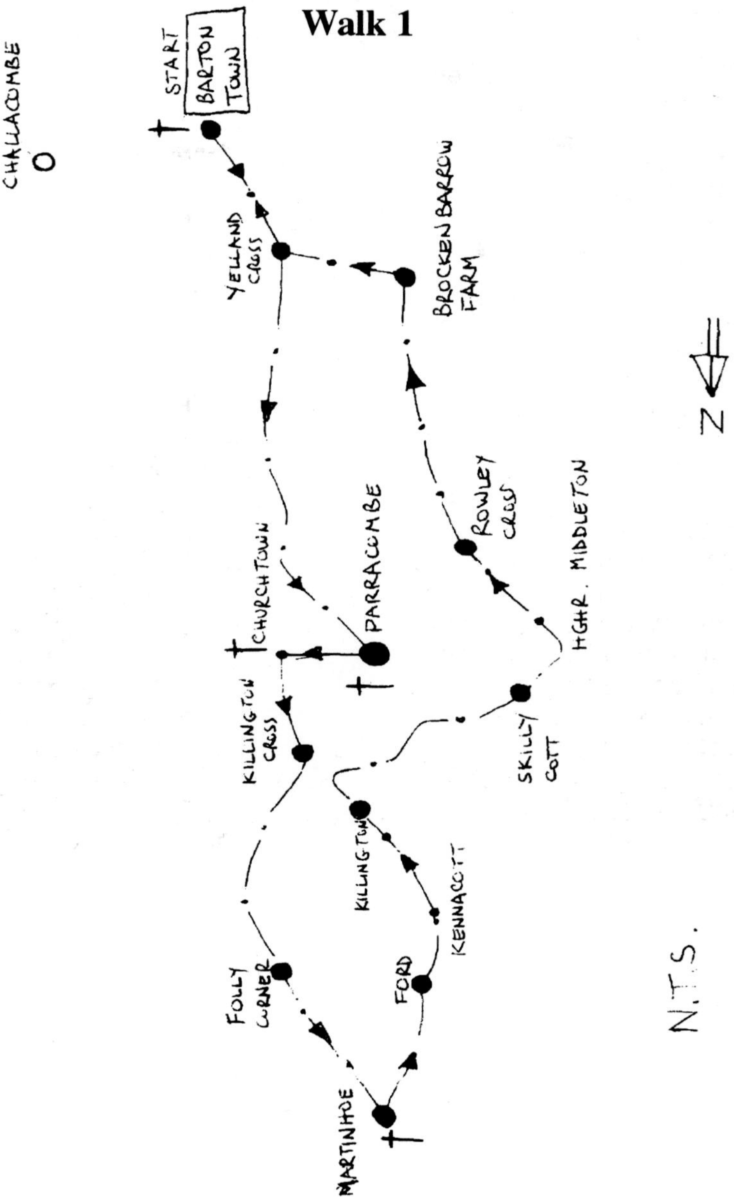

CHALLACOMBE

START
BARTON TOWN

YELLAND CROSS

BROCKEN BARROW FARM

CHURCH TOWN

PARRACOMBE

ROWLEY CROSS

KILLINGTON CROSS

HGHR. MIDDLETON

SKILLY COTT

KILLINGTON

KENNACOTT

FOLLY CORNER

FORD

MARTINHOE

N

N.T.S.

7

CHALLACOMBE.

At the time of viewing, the church was in the hands of builders with the tower shrouded in plastic sheeting. Apparently, it will remain in this condition until mid-1998.

PARRACOMBE.
Christchurch.

This fine old church has for many years been looking after spiritual needs of both Parracombe and Churchtown.

PARRACOMBE.
St. Petrock's.

This church is very old and is no longer used for worship but the fabric is well maintained by the Trust for Historic Churches.

MARTINHOE
St. Martin's.

Old 11th century church with a list of Rectors from 1270. Just inside the gate there is a cluster of graves of the Ridd family. One stone records a lady who lived from 1880 - 1955 whose name was Lorna Doone Ridd. As Lorna Doone was written by R. D. Blackmore in 1869 there is an obvious connection. The population of the parish is now only 150.

Walk No. 2: KENTISBURY - HEALE - TRENTISHOE - DEAN - KENTISBURY

Only 11 miles. One steep climb, otherwise moderate.

Churches: Kentisbury - Trentishoe

Start off at Kentisbury church and walk a short distance along the road to the north and then turn right into what is euphemistically described on the signpost as a bridleway to the A399. Under wet conditions it is quite easy to cross the unofficial ford at the entrance to the track as long as the walker does not mind watery mud up to the ankles. After this baptism by gooey water the going becomes easier and is just ordinary mud until clear of the farm and by the time Silkenworthy Knap is reached boots will be quite clean again. Turn right on to busy A399 for a short distance and then take the signed footpath to the left, to Higher Cowley Farm where a narrow county road is reached. Follow this road past Cowley Wood to Higher East Middleton and the T-junction.

Turn left here into Wheatly Lane and keep going through Heale, bearing right into Invention Wood. The track sweeps round and down (very down) to the left where a footbridge crosses the river from which point follow the signs up (very up) to Trentishoe with its fine old farmhouse and church.

Return by continuing along the county road to the first car park sign on the OS map and turn down to the Ladies Mile Path. Pass Trentishoe Manor (which is almost entirely obscured by trees) and Rudd Cottage and take the footpath through Dean Wood, north to south, which is signposted for Dean. Once in Dean, take the left turn out of the T-junction up to Dean Cross. From Dean Cross proceed with due care and anxiety for just under half a mile to Slade Lane Cross and thence (if you have survived the ordeal) along the lane to Kentisbury. This hazardous journey on the A399 may put a year or two on your life but it does save arriving back at the car with mud up to the ankles as a result of the "ford" referred to above.

This is a short walk but one full of interest. After the initial excitement of the "ford" and once up on the higher ground there are some superb views of the coast and in particular the ravine-like Heddon's Mouth which is such a challenge to walkers of the coast path. On this walk it is crossed much higher up the river at Parsonage Wood but the descent and ascent here are nevertheless quite strenuous. Trentishoe is a delightful hamlet overlooking the sea and owing to its remoteness remains unspoiled by developers. The old farmhouse at Trentishoe is worthy of a photograph as indeed, of course, is the church.

Walk 2

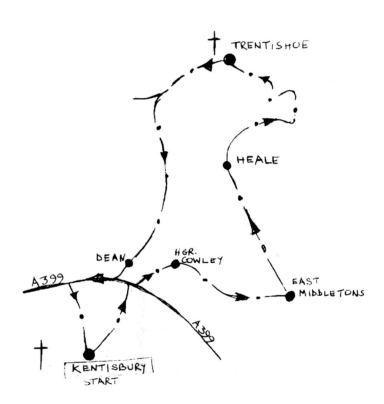

N.T.S.

KENTISBURY.
St. Thomas.

It is a beautiful old church inside and considering how few parishioners it serves, is remarkably spacious.

TRENTISHOE.
St. Peter's.

Like so many of these ancient churches in remote areas it is need of money of repairs for "support the 40" as the notice reads. Apparently in 1891 the population of the church was 96, in 1901 it was 68 and in 1959 had dropped to 40. If our old churches are to survive then some source of finance other than the parishioner will have to be found. In the 1914-18 war, Trentishoe and Martinhoe (150 population) sent 33 local men to serve and in the 1939-45 war, 16. They certainly did their bit.

Walk No. 3. HILLSFORD BRIDGE -WATERSMEET - COUNTISBURY – FORELAND - BLACKGATE - KIPSCOMBE - COAST PATH - LYNMOUTH - HILLSFORD BRIDGE.

13 miles of superb walking

Churches : Countisbury - Lynton

This is one of the shorter walks but one to savour. It has everything - the beautiful Lyn Valley, grand coastal scenery, moorland and as many geological lumps to climb as the average walker will look for in a single day.

Start off at the well sited car park at Hillsford Bridge (southeast of Lynmouth) and walk down the West Lyn to just beyond Watersmeet and then turn off, up and right, on the path to Countisbury which passes through Horners Neck Wood and Trilly. Cross the A39 (ignoring the Sandpiper Inn) and Countisbury lies immediately ahead. At this point join the southwest coastal path but in order to take full advantage of the truly magnificent coastal views carry on right out to Foreland Point and then rejoin the coast path at the head of Caddow Combe. There then lies ahead nearly 2 miles of wild going to Desolation Point where the coast path turns inland to the head of Wingate Combe.

At this point, where the coast path returns to seaward carry straight on following the permitted path shown red on the map. Take the path around Old Barrow Hill to reach the A39 at Black Gate. This is the point of homeward return. Take the path west alongside the A39 to Wingate Farm and pick up the path just east of Dogsworthy and loop around Kipscombe Hill to the farm and press on past Barna Barrow to Countisbury. From here follow the route into Lynmouth. Towards the bottom of Porlock Hill the path is beside the road but there is a good wide wall which is quite safe (safer than the road) to walk on. However, the Park Authority is in the process of rerouting the path to a safer route on the seaward side.

Cross the bridge and turn right into the main part of the village. On this walk it would be advisable to allow anything up to an hour to spend enjoying the amenities. Museums are not normally thought to be necessarily compatible with walking but this one is a must as is the Tourist Centre shop on the front. The Museum has a mass of detail on the disastrous flood of 1952 and the exploits of the people of Lynmouth in the last century when they manhandled a lifeboat up the fearful Porlock Hill in one of the greatest sea rescues of all time. Having done justice to the local amenities return to the Rising Sun beside which a zig zag path ascends apparently to the heavens but in reality to the town of Lynton. The church is easy enough to find and once that visit has been completed return by the path on which ascent was made (it will probably seem easier this time).

Walk back to the coach park and there pick up the path to Watersmeet and Hillsford Bridge. There is an alternative route from Lynmouth to the bridge and that is by means of the Two Moors Way/Tarka Trail. It is a magnificent walk but very much tougher than the one suggested via Watersmeet which itself involves a climb of several hundred feet over 2 miles plus distance. The Two Moors route is only recommended for experienced walkers who have plenty of energy left when they are ready to leave Lynmouth.

Walk 3

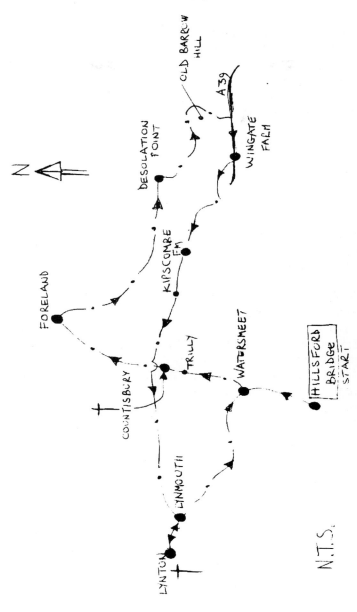

N.T.S.

19

COUNTISBURY.
St. John the Evangelist.

A church with a long history, situated high up above Lynmouth, and familiar sight to walkers along the Southwest Way coast walk.

LYNTON.
St. Mary's.

Another Exmoor church of great interest. There was a church of some sort on the site in Saxon times, but the present structure is about a hundred years old. Perhaps the most striking feature is a list of names which records those who died in the terrible flood of 1952.

Walk No. 4: LYNMOUTH - WATERSMEET - BRENDON - MALMSMEAD - OARE – BRENDON - HILLSFORD BRIDGE - LYNMOUTH

15 miles of glorious walking

Churches: Oare - Brendon.

This one, of all the walks described in this book, is a must - truly a walk for all seasons. It includes the riverside path of the river Lyn up to Watersmeet where the Lyn meets the combined flow of the Farley and Hoaroak Waters and then the entire course of the East Lyn River up to Brendon. The route provides the whole range of variations which Exmoor offers, starting with that absolute gem of a seaside town, Lynmouth, and followed by wooded river valleys and moorland wildness.

In the warm summer months these rivers flow sedately down to the sea with the occasional white race where the gradient is particularly steep but generally in peaceful order. On a hot day the shade from the canopy provided by the extensive oak woods which stretch for several miles is a pleasant relief. In spring and Autumn the colours are quite breathtaking in their intensity and extent but in midwinter it is very different. Noisy flows the Lyn with cascades of miniature waterfalls from numerous points where the steep-sided valley disgorges its runoff into the maelstrom below. The ears are assaulted by an incessant, thunderous roar as the white water thrashes at the rocks, boulders and everything else in its path. With the trees bare at this time of year, the view of the river and the hills becomes more extensive and a wonderful sight it is.

There are two convenient car-parks on entering Lynmouth and this is the place to begin. The walk upstream to Watersmeet is well signed and well trodden by countless feet. Standing at the confluence of the two rivers two very impressive waterfalls on the Farley Water are clearly visible and which make excellent photographs. At Watersmeet, take care to follow the Fisherman's path which begins immediately alongside the Watersmeet house and follows the East Lyn river all the way to Brendon. The Path ends on a county road and the route carries straight on along this road past the entrance to Hall farm for a few yards where a stile on the right-hand side leads to a very steep climb over a considerable distance. Any excess warmth caused by the sheltered walk along the river valley will quickly dissipate as you climb ever higher until you reach the head of Ashton Cleave which is the highest point of the whole walk. The path along this stretch is narrow but clearly marked and it does provide good views of the valley below but nothing as spectacular as the view which meets the eye when turning to descend into the Oare Water Valley. The view looks straight up the steep valley with a great expanse of scree slopes to the left and the Southern wood to the right. From a great height it is a truly magnificent sight. The descent is rapid and the walk proceeds along the north bank of the lovely Oare Water past Oaremead farm and on to Oare.

Take care at the farm because the footpath shown on some maps has been diverted to the northern boundary of the farm itself. This path joins a minor road a matter of a few steps from Oare Church, to the right. Walkers will know they have reached this road when they observe the sign on a field gate opposite which reads, rather ominously, "DO NOT EVEN THINK OF PARKING HERE".
Happily the Oare Church is more welcoming. For visitors to Exmoor who are familiar with R.D. Blackmore's "Lorna Doone", Oare Church is a Mecca since it features so prominently in that novel.

The pilgrimage completed, it is time to turn towards home. Brendon is the first objective and the walker must make a choice between two very different routes. The recollection of the recent climb up from Brendon on the outward journey and the views of Oare Water Valley from the top of Ashton Cleave will probably be fresh in the mind but for those

23

who enjoy a challenge this is the route back.

However, for the more timid (or less masochistic) the roadway is more direct and considerably easier going except that in summer the volume of holiday traffic making its way to and from Oare Church will be a problem at least as far as Malmsmead after which the road is a little wider.

At Malmsmead cross the ancient bridge or paddle through the ford (if the feet are feeling hot). Then either follow the road round to Brendon or take the footpath beside Lorna Doone farm and climb up to Southern Wood, rejoining the road after descending the hill the other side.

Rejoin the footpath from Brendon to Rockford by crossing the bridge at Leeford and turning left. Cross the footbridge opposite the Rockford Inn and passing (or otherwise) the Inn carry on up the rather steep hill for half a mile and arrive at the church and a little further on, the old school house. This walk will give cause to wonder how the children of Brendon and worshippers years ago managed to toil up the hill for a mile and a half in all weathers.

After leaving the church carry on along the road past Crookhorn Gate, turning right at High Gate and right again on reaching the main road. It is all downhill now. The road leads down to Hillsford bridge where the riverside path, all 2 ½ miles of it, to Lynmouth is joined.

Walk 4

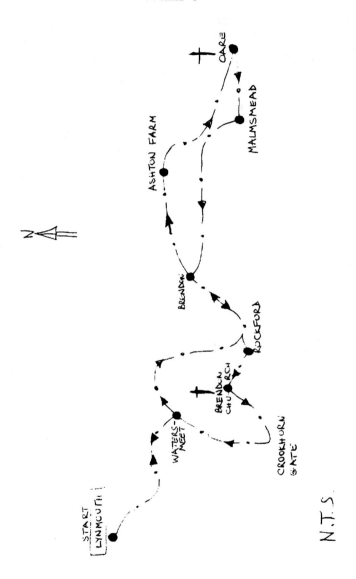

N.T.S.

25

OARE.
St. Mary the Virgin.

This ancient 11th Century church is worth a visit on its own account but the fame arising from Blackmore's book makes it one of the most visited on the moor. What induced the ancients to build a lovely church in this wild and desolate spot is a matter for conjecture but whatever the reason they built well. A tablet on the wall to a Peter Spure 1681 - 1749 is still in excellent condition. There are several fascinating features of this place but having whetted appetites the walker will be left to seek them out for him/herself.

BRENDON.
St. Brendan.

There has been a church in this area since the 12th century but the present structure is of much later origin although it does include certain traces of an earlier one.

Walk No. 5: SOUTH MOLTON - NORTH MOLTON TWITCHEN - MOLLAND - LAMBSCOMBE CROSS - SOUTH MOLTON.

17/18 miles of quite tough walking.

Churches: Twitchen - Molland

This walk is quite different from all the others in the guide but nonetheless interesting and passes through some beautiful Devon countryside. Most of it is just south of the moor itself but is included because Twitchen Church is actually on Exmoor but rather remote from all the others. As South Molton is generally regarded as the gateway to Exmoor it seemed a good idea to include one walk from this lovely old market town and Twitchen was the obvious choice of destination. Molland Church, like West Anstey, is just south of the arbitrary boundary of Exmoor but is so typically Exmoor in character and so close to Twitchen it would have been a shame to omit it. Besides, it makes for a very good walk.

Unfortunately, most of this one is on minor roads and much of it does not appear on the Exmoor leisure map so the enthusiastic walker may find it an advantage to obtain a copy of the OS Pathfinder map 1255 - South Molton which, like the Exmoor map, is at 2 1/2 to the mile. For walkers who prefer not to fill their rucksacks with extra maps the route will be described in some detail.

Park in the large car-park behind the market with the entrance off South-Street and leave the car-park by the exit road (a one-way route into New Road) and turn left for just over 100 yards into the main street (the B3226 which on older maps may still be shown as the A361). Turn right for another 100 yards and then left again into Station Road which after half a mile down the hill meets the North Devon Link Road. Prudence and discretion suggests that a good pause is observed at this junction because it is necessary to

28

cross from one side to the other. As the majority of drivers on the Link-Road seem to be budding formula 1 drivers in training or mistake the 60mph sign as the minimum rather than the maximum speed or even prospective candidates for an early exit from this mortal existence, it is advisable to cross with very great care. There is, in fact, a bridleway which does cross underneath but this is generally severely infested with matted brambles and stinging nettles, so the walker must decide for himself.

Assuming a successful crossing, proceed a few yards along the North Molton road and turn immediately right on to a metalled lane which passes a rather attractive (in modern art terms) scrap metal yard. Half a mile along the lane brings us to Marsh Farm where the track ends and a very pleasant walk beside the river Mole begins and continues the whole way into North Molton. The riverside walk and the hill up into North Molton can be very muddy at times and under these conditions gaiters are desirable. The public footpath emerges on to the road through North Molton and the route is then down to the bridge over the river Mole. At this point the walker will have covered just under 4 miles.

Proceed up the hill, northeast, passing the first right turn near the bridge and trudge up the hill to the second right turning (High Bullen Cross) and take that one. At the junction the Exmoor map comes into its own and shows the route to Twitchen. 3 miles of minor road past the Millbrook Farms, Westland bridge, Kensall Cross and Headgate (Turn right here) leads to a lovely spot - Twitchen Mill with its fine old stone Mill-house still in excellent condition. A short, steep climb brings us into the Hamlet of Twitchen which boasts three public amenities; Church, village hall and a telephone box.

But it is one of those lovely old settlements quite unspoilt by modern building desecration. The Church is in a lovely setting and the Parishioners have thoughtfully provided a bench seat against the south wall where on a warm day its a pleasure to sit for a drink and a bite while enjoying peaceful surroundings and distant views of Exmoor. After the walk from South Molton the refreshment stop will not come amiss.

It is now time to sample the delights of the distant moorland view via the road, southeast which crosses the stream by the unlikely named Bullen's Gruit and climbs up to Cussacombe Common. Continue straight on past the crossroads for a little over half a mile and take the footpath in the field on the right hand side. At the end of the first field the track turns off right but the path to be followed into Molland carries more or less straight on for another half a mile, reaching the road at the west end of the village. Turn left here and just look for the church tower at the far end of the village. In accordance with ancient tradition the church is next to the pub on the basis that there is nothing quite like a refreshing pint after a lusty singsong.

On leaving Molland go back through the village and remain on this road past the point where the footpath joined it and then on to West Molland Barton, where it is a good idea to pause a while to admire the superb Old Manor House and stone farm buildings before proceeding on the same road over Barton Bridge, through Bickingcott Cross, down and up Whitcott Hill to Lambscombe Cross - all very well signposted.

Perhaps at this point it would be helpful to explain that Molland Village does not appear on either of the maps referred to above. There is this small area between the edge of the Exmoor map below Twitchen and the edge of the South Molton map which is on the Pathfinder 1256 DULVERTON map, however in total it involves no more than a mile of walking and is so well signed as to make a map unnecessary.

To return to the route: At Lambscombe Cross turn left and follow this road passing Ley Cross, Limeslake Farm, Bicknor Farm and cross the bridge over the Link-Road, on the corner by the entrance to Pillavin Farm take the footpath across the fields past Windwhistle Farm and emerge on the main road. Cross the Mole bridge and turn immediately left onto Poltimore Road. At the cross road at the top of the hill go straight across and just past the Bowling Green. The car park will be found on the right-hand side.

Walk 5

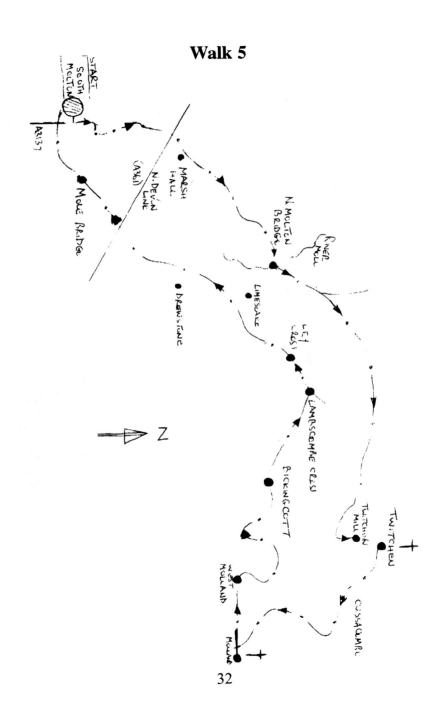

TWITCHEN.
St. Peter's.

Alas! Locked nowadays owing to a number of thefts but it is in a delightful pastoral setting.

MOLLAND.
St. Mary's.

A surprisingly large building considering the size of the Parish but significant enough to be a Grade I listed building. It has the original box pews still in use and has the advantage for parishioners that one has to pass the fine old pub, the London Inn, to reach the church.

Walk No. 6: EXFORD - WITHYPOOL - SIMONSBATH - EXFORD

17/18 miles. An energetic days walking.

Churches : Exford - Withypool - Simonsbath

Start at Exford free car-park. First of all walk back into the village and toil up the steep hill to the right where the Parish Church will be found on the left-hand side of the road. After viewing the church return to the car park. From the car park take the riverside path in a southeast direction, past the Exmoor National Park Depot to Court Farm. Take the path up to Southcott and loop round up the steep climb to Court Copse and then along the Northern boundary of Road Hill. This emerges on to the Room Hill Road but rather than walk on this fast stretch of tarmac it is preferable to walk inside the hedge towards Comer's Cross.

The OS map is not accurate on Room Hill because the footpath shown from the ford at the bottom of Curr Cleave actually continues along the Northern boundary of the hedge shown on the map right out to Room Hill Road. At this junction there is a signpost where the road is crossed and where the sign to Withypool indicates a new footpath not shown on the OS maps. The route is well signed and reaches Withypool just above the village and carries on past (without stopping) the Royal Oak at which point turn North (after viewing the Church) up Kitridge Lane. For about three miles you are now on the two Moors Way taking care to take the most Southerly of the three paths shown on the map. This path gradually descends to the River Barle and Cow Castle by which time you have left the Two Moors Way which crosses the river just before the Castle. Continue along past Wheal Eliza and into Simonsbath.

Leaving Simonsbath after having made the regulatory visit to the church, more or less at the same point as the arrival take the Northern path past Winstitchen Farm and Picked

Stone Quarry and farm. At the farm curve round along the farm road, over the cattle grid, and join the county road above Thornmead turning right and keep to this road for about a mile, turning right at the T junction just before Newland. A short distance down this road there is a track leading through Withycombe Farm which emerges on to the highway again North of Chibbet Post. From Chibbet Post follow the road and short length of footpath back into Exford.

There is an alternative route from Newland due East to Newland Cross thence to South Ley and into Exford along the B3223 but this is not recommended owing to the speed of traffic on this fast stretch of road.

The walk begins with a smart climb up to Road Hill and an equally steep drop into Withypool both of which provide glorious views of the River Exe Valley going up and the Barle Valley on the way down. Simonsbath is an unspoilt village set in beautiful surroundings and has the Exmoor Forest Hotel, one of the most attractive hostelries on the Moor. Wheal Eliza is well worth a minor diversion across the bridge where a board showing the history of the mine is displayed including the sad tale of the mine worker who was hanged for dropping his young daughter down the shaft because he could not afford to keep her.

Walk 6

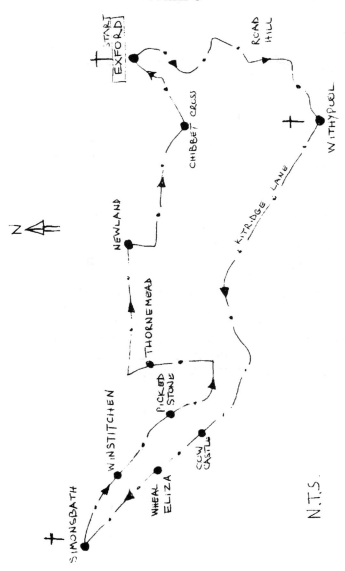

N.T.S.

37

EXFORD.
St. Mary Magdalene.

Situated in a lovely setting the main claim to fame is list of Rectors going back to 1297.

WITHYPOOL.
St. Andrew's.

A great deal of the present building is barely a hundred years old following restoration work by the Victorian "improvers". The tower has been built and rebuilt twice, but the church is still a lovely looking place.

SIMONSBATH.
St. Luke.

This is the Parish Church of Exmoor built in the middle of the 19th Century after Simonsbath became an important centre on Exmoor.

Walk No. 7: EXFORD - EDGCOTT - LARKBARROW CORNER - LUCOTT FARM - LEY HILL - HORNER WOOD - STOKE PERO - EXFORD

15 miles of quite hard walking.

Churches: Stoke Pero.

Start off from Exford free car park - take the county road northwest to Edgcott and branch left to Downscombe caravan site. Just over the stream where the road turns left, carry on up the bridleway to Larkbarrow Corner via Swincombe Cleave. This way emerges onto the highway near Castle Farm. Turn right up to Larkbarrow Corner and then there is a straight three mile trek northwest through Alderman's Barrow, Lucott Cross through to Lucott Farm.

Opposite the farm, there is a very rocky and steep track down to a footbridge over the river. A left turn along the South side of the river brings you to a ford crossing at the caravan site and on to pool Bridge. Continue along the roadway and almost opposite the entrance track to Lucott Farm turn right on the track along the south side of Ley Hill to the entrance to Horner Wood. Follow the footpath down into the woods and at a cross path junction, go straight ahead down the very steep Stags Path. This comes to the Horner water where you turn right for about a third of a mile to the footbridge, cross the bridge and begin the long, steep ascent to Stoke Pero.

Having dallied a while to look at the highest church on Exmoor it is now time to begin the final five mile stretch to Exford. Either follow the county road to Cloutsham Gate or climb up over Stoke Ridge to pick up the road lower down and then carry on up the hill to Lang Combe Head after which it is downhill all the way. Pass Porlock Post and at spot level 432 on the OS map follow the track and then the foot path into Exford.

41

This walk passes through some good deer country particularly the Ley Hill, Cloutsham and Stoke Pero Common areas, so it is useful to have the camera for instant use. This route through the lovely Horner Woods includes the short distance along the track beside Horner Water which is one of the most delightful walks on Exmoor. As it is only accessible by walking to it there is also little chance of it ever becoming overcrowded, an advantage the true walker will appreciate.

Walk 7

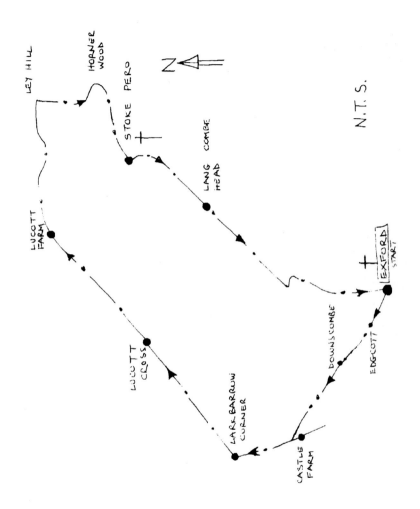

43

STOKE PERO.

Situated at 1013 feet (according to the notice board) above sea level it is claimed to be the highest and most remote church.on Exmoor. At the time of writing work is proceeding on the fabric of the building and a great deal of money is needed still. Having had a good look around this little old church it is easy to think of many less worthy causes for a contribution. The list of rectors goes back to 1242.

Walk No 8. PORLOCK – LUCCOMBE – SELWORTHY – BOSSINGTON – PORLOCK WEIR – CULBONE – PORLOCK WEIR – PORLOCK.

15 miles. A fascinating walk among glorious countryside with breathtaking sea views and several places where the walker will wish to dally.

Churches: Porlock - Luccombe - Selworthy - Culbone.

Park in the central car park in Porlock. Leave the car park by the gate at the southern end and arrive in the main shopping street choked with large volumes of traffic and little or nothing by way of pavements. The church is a short way along after turning left into the town and after spending an appropriate length of time admiring this wonderful old place carry on a little further and turn right to Higher Doverhay.

It is minor road walking for almost all of the five miles to Selworthy but has the advantage of passing through a number of quite unique and unspoilt little hamlets on the way. The first of these is West Luccombe with its old pack horse bridge and where the nearby caravan park is sufficiently detached from the hamlet and well enough sited not to ruin the place.

From West Luccombe follow the road to another gem of a village at Horner where it is even possible to obtain tea and wads in a discreetly located tea room and garden. Continue on towards Luccombe and take the short length of footpath which is signed to Luccombe Church, the object of the exercise. Leaving the church, return along the county road and, ignoring the first road to the right (signed to Minehead), go over the bridge and past East Luccombe Farm. Turn right immediately after the farm and follow the road round to a "T" junction and right again as far as the lodge. Take the road straight on through the white gates from which a

45

very clear view of Selworthy Church is immediately ahead - although some effort is required before arriving there. Follow the gated road up to the last gate which leads on to another "T"-junction and a left turn brings you to the impressive Holnicote House, once the family seat of the Acland family but now alas! a holiday complex.

A short section of footpath leads to a gate on to the fast and furious A39 which has to be crossed - with the utmost care. Immediately opposite is another gate alongside the ochre-coloured Holnicote Cottage which is the start of an attractive footpath up the hill. On reaching the track at the top turn right and amble into Selworthy village where the church is fortunately situated at the far end and thus there is every opportunity to savour the delights of what must be one of the most beautiful villages in England. Evidently, the Acland family were first class landowners who have left posterity a superb example of a well-managed estate. The group of thatched cottages and the old tithe barn must make many an American tourist drool with ecstasy! The Church itself is an equally fine example of historic interest and as a matter of interest, with its white walls against a dark green background is visible from miles away on various places on Exmoor, making a very good landmark. The village itself is now National Trust property and should therefore remain unspoiled for all time.

The first time visitor will want to spend quite a time in Selworthy so any planning should take this into account Once the appreciation appetite is sated, it will be time to move on and start retracing steps along the Selworthy to Allerford track which is clearly marked on the map. At Allerford take the road down into Bossington and pick up the South West Coast Path which follows the beach all the way to Porlock Weir. Although flat as a pancake, this mile and a half will be as hard and uncomfortable as any encountered on any of the walks in this guide. Just be sure not to be wearing plimsolls or carpet slippers!

Porlock Weir is yet another fascinating little seaside place full of character and boasting a fine hostelry, The Anchor Hotel. A pause here will enable the walker to recover breath and composure before beginning the assault on Yearner Wood. The coast path is joined just behind the Anchor Hotel and is then clearly marked across the fields up to the road at Worthy Manor. Thereafter simply follow the sign to Culbone Church. Although following the signs is a simple matter, be prepared for a long, steep haul up through the woods. The walk is lovely at any time of the year but winter does have the advantage of glorious sea views when the trees are without leaf. Culbone is an odd place to build a church (at least it appears so) but no doubt the ancients knew what they were about. Anyone making the journey up from Porlock Weir will consider the effort involved well worth it when they see this delightful little cluster of old houses and church. Small as Culbone is, someone has had the foresight or entrepreneurial acumen to put up a small refreshment hut for the benefit of passing walkers. It does of course lie on the South West Way (or South West Coast Path as the OS map names it) and the path is very well used.

The return journey is a case of retracing steps as far as Worthy (which will take a good deal less time than it did going up). At Worthy, ignore the acorn sign (a South West Way logo) and keep going along the road to Porlockford. Leave the road here and pick up the sign on the right that points the route of a footpath to West Porlock and all the way to Porlock itself without the necessity to use the narrow and very busy road. At Porlock the path ends at a road just above Court Place and it is then just a matter of carrying on into the town and locating the central car park.

Walk 8

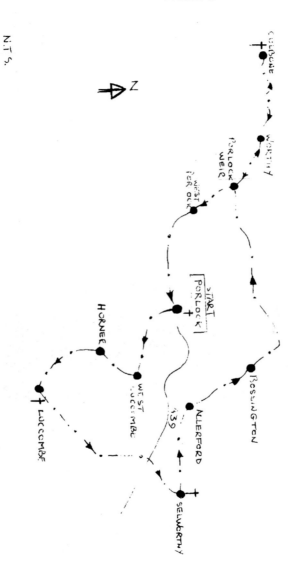

N.T.S.

N

COLEBORNE

WORTHY

PORLOCK WEIR

WEST PORLOCK

START
PORLOCK

HORNER

WEST LUCCOMBE

BOSSINGTON

ALLERFORD

139

LUCCOMBE

SELWORTHY

PORLOCK.
St. Dubricius.

A Welsh Saint. Beautifully maintained and a pleasure to look around. The list of rectors, like so many of these Exmoor Churches, goes back a long way, in this case to 1297. An interesting feature of the war memorial plate is the name among those killed in the 1939-45 war of Lt. Cdr. Arkwright RN, because a brass plate commemorating him is on the wall of Culbone church as well and Culbone is a different parish.

LUCCOMBE.
St. Mary the Virgin.

For a parish numbering just 100 souls this is a truly magnificent church which has evidently served bigger congregations in the past. The leaflet in the church (20p) sets out the history of St. Mary's and makes interesting reading.

SELWORTHY.
All Saints.

The steepish climb to get here will be soon forgotten on entering this absolute gem of a church. The Acland family who were so prominent in the area and bequeathed large areas of Exmoor (including Dunkery Beacon) to the National Trust figure prominently on the marble tablets round the walls. Money is required for repairs now but the problem is not apparent to the casual visitor.

CULBONE.
St. Beuno.

Apparently the name of another Welsh Saint. This tiny church (it can, as a notice reads, seat 39 people in great discomfort!) is not only mentioned in, the Doomsday Book but in the more up to date publication, The Guinness Book of Records. Its claim to fame arises from the fact that it is reckoned to be the smallest complete church in England. The visitor will feel uplifted and very pleased to have made the pilgrimage to this lovely little place.

Walk No 9: WHEDDON CROSS - CUTCOMBE - CHURCHTOWN - TIMBERSCOMBE - WOOTTON COURTENAY - PUTHAM FORD - WHEDDON CROSS.

16 miles. A good day's country walk with magnificent scenery and occasional views of high moor.

Churches: Cutcombe - Churchtown - Timberscombe - Wootton Courtenay

There is a very good free car park at the rear of the Rest and be Thankful (but not until the walk is completed). Cross the busy main road with care and take the minor road to Cutcombe. Pass right through (fairly quickly) this most uninspiring of villages to enjoy a good look at the lovely old church with the glorious expanse of scenery to the south.

Return a short distance back along the approach road and turn left at the fork to Cutcombe Cross. Carry on straight across to join the slippery and very rough track which rises towards Lype Hill. Pause awhile on the way up to look back at the superb view of Dunkery Beacon and surrounding moorland. Pass through Pitleigh Kennels (keeping the dog on a lead by request) and keep to the blue markers up to the top of Lype Hill.

At this point the map is not strictly accurate. The path is through the gateway to the left of the compound containing the OS Trig. point - not right as shown. Ignoring the map, make for the stile at the north east corner of the field having gone through the gateway and then follow the yellow markers along the top side of the fence. This carries on until it seems to disappear at a spot where the farmer has constructed a most elaborate water distribution arrangement. A little way up the fence line at right angles in front of you there is a gateway with a blue sign which confirms you are back on the straight and narrow. Drop down to the fence line and continue alongside it all the way to the head of a very steep rough track which eventually emerges at Westcott Farm. Note that nothing less than good stout footwear is adequate for this descent. The views on the way down are superb and Churchtown appears as a birds eye view.

Turn right on the track which leads down to the county road and proceed a little way down towards Luxborough in order to see the church. Unlike Cutcombe earlier, Churchtown is a most attractive little settlement in a glorious rural setting.

For the gourmet and those walkers whose love of exercise is matched by a natural disposition to gourmandry there is a first class inn down in Luxborough itself. However, it must be stressed that the round trip for those seeking The Royal Oak is just under a mile with the return journey to Churchtown involving a severe hill climb which is not generally a good prospect after having indulged in refreshment,

The more sober minded will retrace their steps from the church to Butcher's Farm and turn right up the path signed to Croydon Hill. In fact, once through the first field the path opens out into a broad expanse of grass road which rises to Croydon Woods. Once again a look behind on the way up is rewarding because the view will include the whole of the steep drop into Churchtown on the other side of the valley.

On reaching the bridleway signed for Timberscombe take this wide metalled track for about a mile where it meets the county road and a few yards along on the left hand side continue on the bridleway to Timberscombe. About half a mile along the track a gateway on the left hand side has a blue mark. Turn in here and follow the fence all the way down to the gate at the bottom. Through the gate, turn half right and go down over the field to meet the fence at the bottom. Right here will eventually emerge at a sort of farmyard that is not only badly surfaced but the first gateway is a morass of messy gunge of doubtful origin when conditions are wet. However, having cleared the second gateway turn left down the track which leads into Timberscombe.

Timberscombe is another lovely little village boasting another fine hostelry, The Lion Inn, which you should pass en route for the church of St. Petrock's.

After leaving the church drop down to the main road and look ,for the sign indicating the footpath to Wootton Courtenay. This is well signed throughout and is just a pleasant cross country stroll along the valley. Turn right into the village and make straight for the church (there is little else of interest in the place). Following the usual inspection, turn back along the road but this time carry straight on past Burrow Farm to Harwood Cross. Although entirely on tarmac this mile or so is pleasant enough walking. At Harwood Cross, turn left to meet the main A396 and turn right for a short (but possibly exciting) distance before leaving the A396 to the budding grand-prix drivers at Pitt Bridge. There follows a stiff climb all the way up to Slade Farm. Take this very rough track for about half a mile where it reaches the county road and after turning right for a short distance, turn right again down the lane to Stowey Farm. At the farm have a camera ready for some good photographs of old buildings. From Stowey Farm the route meanders down past Kersham to Putham Ford and this section is probably the most wonderful of the whole trip, it really is rural England at its very best.

Having crossed Putham Ford either by paddling or over the stone bridge the last mile of the walk lies ahead. Perhaps it is not good planning to end the day with the most savage climb up a terrible RUPP with its stream and outcropping rocks definitely not suitable for the baby's pushchair. However, in the words of one of my walking companions, "if it's gotta be done...." And alas! it has. The climb does eventually come to an end. After Putham Lane, straight across Cutcombe Cross and along Popery Lane, Wheddon Cross appears as a most welcome (and be thankful) sight. The average walker will know he/she has had a good day out.

Walk 9

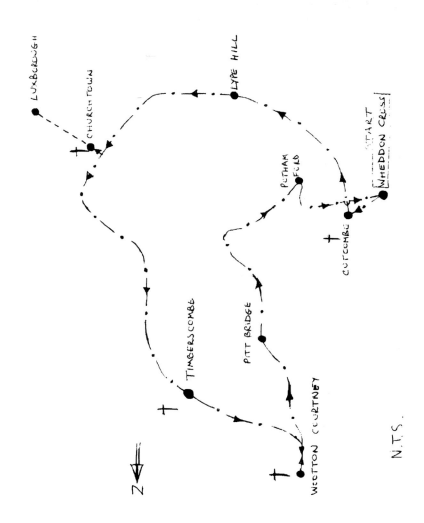

CUTCOMBE.
St. John the Evangelist.

Evidently a great mix of various architectural styles but lovely inside. It is described as "typical of small country churches of hill districts of Exmoor". It has a very ornate 12th century font just inside the door. At the time of writing the whole church was bedecked in a beautifully colourful display of Easter flowers.

CHURCHTOWN.
St. Mary's.

*St. Mary's is the parish Church of Luxborough, set in a delightful village,
which dates back to Norman times.*

TIMBERSCOMBE.
St. Petrock's.

The origins are apparently lost in the mists of time but seem to pre-date the Conquest. The church and churchyard are kept in immaculate condition in keeping with the village as a whole.

WOOTTON COURTENAY
All Saints.

The village itself is the sort of place that is quite a pleasure to drive through (without stopping) but the church is well worth a visit. Although the 19th century improvers have done their worst the interior remains elegant and well maintained. The list of rectors goes back to 1311.

Walk No. 10: DULVERTON - BRIDGETOWN - EXTON - WINSFORD - DULVERTON

Approx. 15 miles with some quite difficult hills to negotiate.

Churches: Dulverton - Exton - Winsford

Commence at one of two Dulverton car parks and having contributed the £1.20 or so to the voracious Pay & Display meter, go straight up to the church and enjoy a degree of spiritual uplift prior to starting the walk proper. This could be helpful because the first half mile or so up past the school to the north and the track up through Weir Cleeve is very steep. It does level out to some extent before reaching the "T"-junction at Higher Broford but it is quite hard work particularly in wet weather when the surface is extremely messy,

On reaching the "T"-junction, turn right a short way, then left followed soon after by yet another right turn and then follow the roadway up to the point where the road itself turns sharp right down into Broford Farm. The route is clearly shown on the OS map and is not difficult to follow. Anyone with a good nose for the delicate fragrances of the countryside will know they are on the right track when passing the huge silage pit situated among a miscellaneous collection of farm buildings and impedimenta.

Where the road turns into the farm, leave the tarmac and go through the gate immediately in front of you. There is a sign by the gatepost but it is overgrown and difficult to see, however, the map does show the footpath very accurately and by following it beside the hedges you will arrive at a farm gate at the entrance to Broford Woods. This gate has long since abandoned all ambition to ever move again so be prepared to jump over it. The woodland walk is lovely but care is needed to turn right at the point shown on the map so that you can cross the stream by a footbridge where the map shows a ford.

Once across the stream take the central (northerly) tarmac lane past Hollam Farm and on into Bridgetown Plantation. From the top of the hill there is a fine view of Bridgetown and by following the markers you are soon down into the village on the West side of the River Exe. Turn right on reaching the minor road and cross the river via the road bridge from which point one has a splendid view of the caravan site and the back gardens of a row of council houses.

Bridgetown is in fact a pleasant enough village and boasts a fine looking pub (The Badgers Holt) which the writer has passed on numerous occasions but always without stopping (an oversight which will certainly be put right one day). The village does have one disadvantage in that it lies on the very busy Dulverton to Minehead road (A396) which carries a great deal of holiday traffic.

After partaking of such amenities as the walker wishes it is necessary to turn left onto the A396 for a very short distance before turning on to the side road marked "Exton" on the right hand side. The relief at having left the traffic behind is soon forgotten in the effort to mount this very steep hill which eventually brings you to the object of the exercise, namely Exton Church. Exton itself is something of a nothingness sort of place but pleasant enough in its way and it does have the advantage over Bridgetown in that it is wonderfully peaceful. The 1,000 year old church is one of the loveliest of them all and is well worth a lengthy break in the journey.

After physical as well as spiritual refreshment leave the church behind and follow the RUPP (in wet weather "wallow" would be a more appropriate term) which emerges on to the A396 a short distance from Coppleham Cross. Turn left at the junction (it is hardly a cross) over Week Bridge and take the path to the North West up yet another very steep hill but with rewarding views. At the entrance to West Hometown is a cross paths junction with the one to the right signed "Battleton Brake" this is the one to take up past Upcott and so on to Upcott lane. Turn left here to Upcott Cross and enjoy the steep downhill walk along Furzehill Lane.

A short walk along the Exford Road brings you into the delightful village of Winsford. Make straight for the church and then to matters practical. Winsford is the ideal place to pause for refreshment of whatever sort the walker prefers. There is a splendid (if rather expensive pub), the Royal Oak, newly rebuilt after a disastrous fire a couple of years ago, where all manner of delights are on offer but there is also a little cafe with a large tea garden down beside the river for those of less exotic tastes. However, for the dedicated walker there is a small area of green right in the village centre where on a sunny day it is a pleasure to sit sipping water and munching a sandwich while watching the touristy world go by.

For students of history there is a house in the village which proudly displays a plaque commemorating the fact that Ernest Bevin, the elder statesman, and one time Foreign Secretary, was born there in 1881.

Chez Bevin is passed as you make your way along the Edbrooke Road as far as Edbrooke Mill House where it is advisable to take a very deep breath because the severest test of the walk lies before you. Follow the Oh! so steep Edbrooke Hill (track) all the way up to Edbrooke Hill Gate at which point the worst of the days travails are behind you.

Follow the Leigh Lane South all the way to the "T" junction at Higher Broford only this time turn right and proceed back towards Dulverton. For the very keen, there is a superb alternative route to Higher Broford which turns off Leigh Lane just South of Summerway and crosses a number of fields although most walkers will find the Leigh Lane preferable by this time.

Having turned right at this point retrace steps Southwards as far as the point where a RUPP to the right by the impressive name of Loosehall Lane begins. There is a clear signpost here and tree lovers will notice the magnificent clump of majestic fir trees at the junction of the ways. A precipitous drop via a very rough path soon emerges at Marsh Bridge where the River Barle is crossed via the lovely old iron bridge. From Marsh Bridge the path is mainly a superb riverside walk all the way into Dulverton and journeys end.

Walk 10

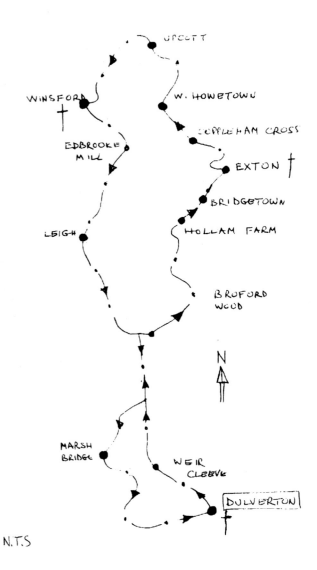

UPCOTT

W. HOWETOWN

WINSFORD

COPPLEHAM CROSS

EDBROOKE MILL

EXTON

BRIDGETOWN

HOLLAM FARM

LEIGH

BROFORD WOOD

N

MARSH BRIDGE

WEIR CLEEVE

DULVERTON

N.T.S

66

DULVERTON.
All Saints Church.

Is quite a large building and, not surprisingly, is well maintained but being more of a town church it lacks the intimacy of the smaller, moorland churches. In the early spring the entire churchyard is a glorious show of daffodils and crocus.

EXTON.
St. Peter.

This 1,000 year old church is quite fascinating and probably one of the loveliest of them all. It has a list of Incumbents going back to 1314 one of whom, The Rev. Warren, served no less than 59 years from 1864 - 1923 - he evidently liked the place. The church is clearly an important part of the village life. There are memorials to many local men who have been killed in wars. In the 1914-18 war no less than 36 men from the parish enlisted including four Broadens and four Quarterlays. Only one of these eight was among the eight unfortunate men who did not return. At present time the church is endeavouring to raise £25,000 towards essential repairs to the tower (a rather familiar story) and has adopted the novel idea of inviting visitors to "buy a brick or tile" for £1.

WINSFORD.
St. Mary Magdalene.

The old stone walls were covered in rendering years ago which now looks somewhat run down but inside the visitor is treated to a feast of history. The list of vicars goes back to the 13th century and early entries suggest all was not well in Winsford. In 1310 a certain Willelmus, a blind vicar, was in office but it seems the two succeeding incumbents refused to pay the blind man 100 shillings (£5) a year pension!. His grievance is on record for all posterity to see. Unusually there is also a list of church wardens dating back from 1551 and like the list of Vicars is maintained in impeccable condition. A tablet on the wall is in memory of the Edbrooke family, dated 1894 and refers to the three centuries during which the family were local landowners. A nice touch is the displaying the dead of the two world wars with a wreath of poppies underneath. Apparently there is a rota of parishioners who look after the memorial and keep it fresh.

Walk No. 11: DULVERTON - MARSH BRIDGE - HAWKRIDGE - ANSTEY GATE - WEST ANSTEY ~ EAST LISCOMBE - DULVERTON.

A full 15 miles of moderate walking.

Churches: Hawkridge - West Anstey.

Starting at Dulverton. Park in the very expensive, but convenient, car park opposite the National Park Office which is situated on the bank of the River Barle. The car park is free in winter.

Cross the river by the main road bridge and follow the sign to Marsh Bridge and Hawkridge along the West bank of the river. This is a lovely walk with woods on one side and the river on the other. It is also the only easy walking of the day. From Hawkridge to Anstey Gate navigational care is needed. Taking the county road southwest for a short distance, turn off at West Hollowcombe and cross the field then another road and continue to Zeal Farm. At certain times of the year the Dane's Brook is fordable with dry feet, at others some prancing from stone to stone (usually with at least one wet foot) is necessary and during the Monsoon season a dry crossing is possible by selecting a suitable branch of an overhanging tree and crossing 'a la Tarzan. This can cause a flask of coffee to leak into the sandwiches or temporarily dislocate the back (or the liver) but at least the feet keep dry. Anyway, having somehow or other crossed the river find the route over Anstey Rhiney Moor to Anstey Gate. This is not immediately apparent and an occasional glance at the compass might well avoid an unscheduled diversion.

At Anstey Gate follow the footpath west until a cross-paths is reached and then turn South to spot level 286. Proceed for about a mile past Ringcombe and Woodland Plantations and turn off to Woodland Farm at the cattle grid on the county road. From the farm the path crosses the stream in the valley and climbs to Churchtown Farm beside West Anstey Church. This church is actually about half a mile South of the park boundary but is so typically Exmoor in character it has been included in this guide. In fact for the next three miles or so the walk is South of the National Park but it does provide for some exciting walking. The section to Badlake Farm (have the camera ready here for a photo of a beautiful old farmhouse) and down to the footbridges over the stream is innocuous enough and fun begins thereafter. For a considerable distance the "lane" is fairly wet most times in the year but after prolonged rainfall it is more like a tributary of the Barle when it would be handy to have a snorkel or a Bailey Bridge in the rucksack.

On one walk the writer had to collect big stones from the vicinity on two occasions in order to construct crossings of streams flowing across the track. In a third place it was necessary to make a diversion over a field and make an à la Tarzan type crossing from a convenient tree. All of which adds to the excitement of a day's walk - you have been warned.

Once through the East Anstey swamps and the Liscombes it becomes plain sailing by following the path through Higher Chilcott and Old Berry Farm into Dulverton.
This walk has a great deal of variety. The walker begins with the woodland/waterside section, followed by open moorland and finally opens, rolling countryside - not to mention the mud.

Walk 11

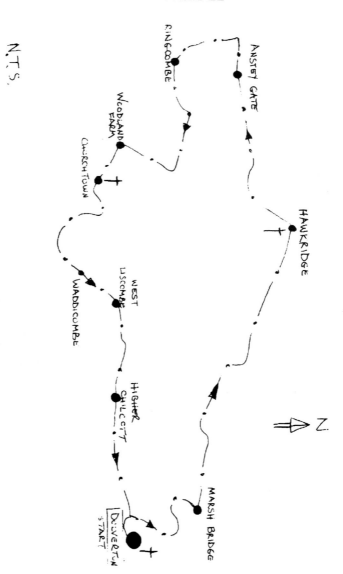

N.T.S.

RINGCOMBE
ANSTEY GATE
WOODLAND FARM
CHURCHTOWN
HAWKRIDGE
WEST LISCOMBE
WADDICOMBE
HIGHER CHILCOTT
MARSH BRIDGE
DULVERTON START

N.

HAWKRIDGE.
St. Giles.

A small church and much restoration has taken place but it retains a most attractive south doorway.

WEST ANSTEY.
St. Petrocks.

Although not strictly speaking an Exmoor church, it is close enough and sufficiently typical to be included.

Walk No. 12: WIMBLEBALL LAKE RESERVOIR CAR PARK (South East of Brompton Regis and near the sailing club) - BROMPTON REGIS - YOUNG'S LINHAY - GOOSEMOOR FARM - GUPWORTHY FARM - FORD HOLLOW - WITHIEL FLOREY - COPHOLE FARM - BESSOM CROSS - Round the Lake - Car park.

16 miles of moderate walking with a lake for a bonus.

Churches: Brompton Regis - Withiel Florey

Leave the car park and turn right for a short distance and then turn left on to the footpath sign-posted Brompton Regis. It is a wild and wet path down to the stream which is crossed by a foot bridge (if the preceding bog has not swallowed you up). Thereafter the path is very good and is well marked throughout.

Emerging on to the road above Pulhams Mill proceed straight on into Brompton Regis and visit the church before taking the Footpath to Kennisham Hill which runs more or less North for nearly two miles. Care is needed in the descent to the stream owing to outcropping rock which when wet will test any nonslip boot soles for efficiency. The walk beside the stream is very attractive but only extends a relatively short distance when a signpost to Kennisham Hill takes a steep climb to the right and up to a large and prominent chunk of rock. Even if the climb has not left you breathless it is a good idea to pause here and look back towards Brompton Regis down the valley - it is a glorious sight.

The sign leads up to a decaying stile and then to three old beech trees part way up the hill. Keep on North from here keeping to the east side of the hedge as far as it goes and then strike across the field to Young's Linhay. The path eventually meets a bridleway crossing at right angles but the route to follow is straight on. So far all the markers have been in yellow but at this point they change to bridleway blue, but are just as easy to follow. A short distance further the path joins a track which serves Leigh Farm to the right but this walk continues North all the way along the track to the county road.

On reaching the road turn right for a few yards and leave the road via a footpath down across the fields. There are no markers on this stretch until the path arrives at a point which looks down on Gupworthy Farm, however, the OS map shows the route clearly enough and no problems should arise. Pass through the farm and on reaching the road turn right for a few hundred yards and take the left hand roadway at the T junction. TAKE CARE HERE. The OS map names the first farm FORD FARM but this is no longer correct. The new name is FORD HOLLOW and FORD FARM is now situated half a mile further along just before reaching Withiel Farm. The point is stressed because the walker is likely to be confused on seeing the name Ford Farm half a mile from where it should be according to the map.

Having arrived safely at the new Ford Farm follow the roadway around and at the T junction turn right and continue straight on to Withiel Florey and the church.

There is a stile at the Southern boundary of the churchyard which leads onto the path going due South to Cophole Farm. (There are no signs at all on this half mile stretch until the county road is reached at Cophole Farm - when the North to South walker has no need of any). Once over the stile at the church, turn half left which takes you down the steep hill to another stile leading into Edgerton Plantation. The short length down to the stream is very overgrown and also very steep with a barbed wire fence on the right hand side, so care is needed. After crossing the stream there is a very steep section which again is very rough going until clear of the wood. The last part past the farm is quite easy going and a right turn along the highway gives a half mile down-hill stroll to Bessom Bridge. On the near side of the bridge turn sharp left and crossing the causeway begin the seven mile trek around the lake. One advantage of walking the edge of the lake is the fact that one cannot get lost and so proceed to follow the path all the way round and back to the car park. The route is naturally well defined and in most places quite reasonable although the section below Upton Farm and South Hill Wood is very lumpy.

The dam is a huge structure and the walker will certainly wish to dally here awhile to admire the surroundings and no doubt add to the photo tally. The walk overall is lovely country rather than true moorland but it does offer some beautiful views and water is always an attraction - Wimbleball Lake is no exception.

Walk 12

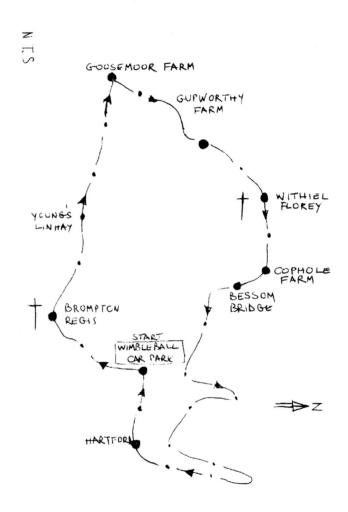

BROMPTON REGIS.
St. Mary the Virgin.

It has some lovely old features but suffered considerable misfortune as a result of the efforts of Victorian "improvers" but is nevertheless still a fine old building. The present church dates from the 13th Century but it is believed there was a Saxon church on the site originally. The list of Vicars commences with Willelm Hawkedon in 1270. A tablet to the Dyke family dating from 1606-1654 and a more recent tapestry of the Last Supper are both in excellent condition.

WITHIEL FLOREY.
St. Mary Magdalene.

A most unusual and interesting church both in external appearance and internally as well. The inside is lit by a number of most attractive oil lamps which no doubt help to keep the temperature up for winter worshippers. The unusual feature of the inside is the lack of memorials compared with most Parish Churches. Apart from two large tablets beside the altar displaying the Ten Commandments (almost legible) and a tablet over the organ (totally illegible) there is just one to an old huntsman of the last century and this plate is burnished bright and clear. Otherwise the walls are bare.

Walk No: 13: DUNSTER (Main Car Park) - GALLOX BRIDGE - CARHAMPTON GATE - BRIDDICOTT FARM - WITHYCOMBE – RODHUISH - GOLSONCOTT - ROADWATER - GLASSES FARM - FELONS OAK – MONKSLADE - WITHYCOMBE HILL GATE - DUNSTER.

14 miles of moderate walking offering extensive views of lush countryside.

Churches: Dunster - Withycombe - Roadwater.

Allow as much time as possible either before commencing the walk or at the end in order to enjoy some of the interesting features of this beautiful old town. There are two car parks (both expensive) in Dunster with the church equidistant between them so one takes one's pick. This walk is written up assuming the higher park is the starting point.

The main street gives the appearance of having cars parked everywhere, the number only being exceeded by the plethora of "Tea-Shoppe's" all the way down. However, the old market cross and the view of the castle towering over the town makes it all worthwhile.

The church is easily found and after spending the necessary time to fully appreciate this glorious place, continue down the main street and turn left into Mill Lane. The walk down to the Gallox Bridge is through a group of well-kept cottages in an old world setting to the stream which is crossed by means of the old stone bridge leading to the superb parkland scenery of Dunster Park. Take the path southwest to Carhampton Gate which is clearly signposted to this point but the path to Aller Farm is not at all clear. The OS map shows the path crossing the middle of a field but there is no visible indication on the ground. The best way is to continue along Park lane and go into the field via the gate at the southern end, then keep to the edge of the field until arriving at the end of the lane which leads into Aller Farm. Passing south of the farm follow the route shown on the map and pick up the beginning of the lane that then continues through Briddicott Farm (gum boot and a deodorant spray could be useful here) as far as Hill Lane. A left turn followed very quickly by a right turn over a stile leads across fields to Withycombe Lane (West Street according to the street sign) and down the hill into the village of Withycombe. Pretty enough in its way it is unexceptional compared with other Exmoor villages of the same size although the local inhabitants may well challenge the description. The vicar would seem to be somewhat bashful or reticent because the church is kept locked and there is no notice to even tell the visitor who the Patron Saint happens to be.

After a rather brief stop in Withycombe, press on up the Higher Rodhuish road into the hamlet of Rodhuish itself which has almost as much to commend it as does Withycombe. Pass swiftly through the place past Styles Farm (where ice-cream is produced commercially), Lower Rodhuish Farm and carry straight on. Follow the county road around the right-angled bend to the Lodge, turn left to Forche's Gardens and then right into Golsoncott. Just south of the farm a footpath begins on the left hand-side of the road and following the right-hand route at the fork (not the one to Lower Roadwater) the walker emerges onto the road immediately beside the church in Roadwater.

This is the limit of the outward journey so, after such time as is necessary to view the church begin the homeward trek by the roadway to the south past the excellent hostelry stoutly named "The Valiant Soldier' (relative to the size of Roadwater the pub seems huge as well as very good) as far as Glasses Farm. A short distance past the farm a footpath to the right crosses the stream and continues up through the wood and across a field. Turn left as shown on the OS map and follow the hedge along the edge of one field and turn up to Croydon Hill School which is a truly magnificent building set in lovely grounds and the walker who is interested in photography will certainly want a photo or two here.

After duly admiring the school carry on up to Felon's Oak and turn left keeping straight on for a good mile and a half to Monkslade Common. Take the track to the north outside of the woods past Rodhuish Common, Red Girt and then on to Withycombe Hill Gate. From here it is all downhill into Dunster Park and Gallox Bridge followed by the uphill stint up through the town to the car park. For the thirsty walker there is no shortage of liquid refreshment in Dunster town.

Walk 13

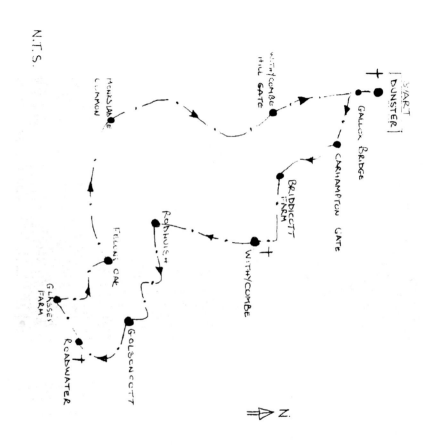

N.T.S.

START
[DUNSTER]

GALLOX BRIDGE

CARHAMPTON GATE

WITHYCOMBE
HILL GATE

MONKSLADE
COMMON

BRIDDICUTT
FARM

WITHYCOMBE

ROBHUISH

FELONS OAK

GLASSES
FARM

GOLSONCOTT

ROADWATER

N.

DUNSTER.
St. George

The Parish and Priory Church of St. George. Probably the grandest of all the churches included in this guide. Like Dunster itself St. George's is steeped in history and the visitor will want to spend time absorbing some of it.

WITHYCOMBE.

After St. George's this small Parish Church could hardly be anything but ordinary but no doubt once inside the air of peace and calm common to all these churches would be evident.

ROADWATER.

A rather unusual sort of place. From the outside it vaguely resembles a church but inside looks more like a village hall and this one does lack the atmosphere common to all the others.

Walk No: 14: TREBOROUGH - LEIGHLAND CHAPEL – NETTLECOMBE - MONKSILVER - ELWORTHY - MONKSILVER - BIRDS HILL - TREBOROUGH.

16 miles of excellent walking through the superb rolling countryside of the Brendon hills with exquisite little hamlets and villages.

Churches: Treborough - Leighland - Nettlecombe - Monksilver - Elworthy.

There is plenty of good parking in the tiny hamlet of Treborough although it is good manners to ask one of the two or three householders where the most convenient place would be. Of course, it is first of all necessary to find Treborough and a little careful navigation maybe required to avoid arriving hot and bothered!

Having arrived safely and being fully booted and spurred, either have a look at the church before setting out or leave until the other end of the day. Return to the "main" Roadwater road and immediately opposite is a gate with a FP sign which is the start of the path to Stamborough. The route indicated on the OS map is accurate so follow it carefully because the next indication of a footpath is a stile at the entrance to the southern end of Treborough Wood. Follow the path round and leave the wood by another stile and through the gateway on the left which one can hardly miss because it has a sign "Bull in the Field" prominently displayed. The field is a very large one so there would be ample notice of any rampaging bulls moving towards you. A survey of the area suggests there is no practical alternative to the official path which does place the nervous walker firmly on the horns of a dilemma. However, there is no need for undue concern about it providing he/she can clear a four foot barbed wire fence and has no prickly feelings

Stamborough. Shortly afterwards the rather attractive little settlement of Leighland Chapel is reached with (in spite of the "Chapel" name) the "Parish Church of Leighland" standing proudly in its midst. This does appear somewhat curious because according to the OS map there is civil parish of Leighland yet the church is described as above.Something perhaps for the walker/Sleuth to investigate.

On leaving the church the path lies right ahead and a left turn down through the churchyard leads on to a short walk to Pitt Mill Farm. Follow the path up into Pitt Wood and after a short climb join the wide track and bridleway and follow the sign to Chidgley, another pretty little place. At Chidgley Farm the path leads north-east to Nettlecombe and the third church of the day. The approach through Nettlecombe park gives a beautiful view of Nettlecombe Court with the church immediately opposite. The Court is now a field centre but the whole place reeks of history and it is well worth arranging to spend a little extra time in order to enjoy the fascinating old family seat.

A quiet leafy lane leads to Woodford and to a footpath to Monksilver, which runs parallel to the road, but to the south of it. The path is a straightforward plod through fields but the far end as it reaches Monksilver can be rather overgrown and painful if the brambles are in season.

The church guide describes the church as a little gem, an apt description which applies equally to the village with its old stone and thatched cottages all in excellent condition. This is the biggest place to be encountered on the walk and the only one to boast a pub, the Notley Arms, which looks disturbingly enticing. However, for the dedicated walker temptation must be resisted because there is a-long way to go yet. The stretch to Elworthy involves a climb up to Combe Cross Lane, thence to Combes Cross, Silvertown Hill and Maunsborough Lane. Take care not to miss the right turn which starts the very rough and very steep drop into Elworthy itself and to the church.

It is difficult to imagine how small a place could ever have supported a church and it is no suprise to find it is on the list of redundant churches or that services are no longer held there.

Elworthy is the furthest point of the walk and it is now a matter of re-tracing steps to Monksilver by one of two routes. The quieter of the two is by toiling back up the RUPP but a more scenic and interesting way is by road (B3188) along the valley. Road walking is not usually recommended but is not too busy and offers splendid views of both the valley and the charming old farmhouse at Combe Sydenham.

From Monksilver take the southerly path which climbs via Bird's Hill to Colton Cross. The long, steady climb may present no problem to a bird but to Homo Sapiens, with two feet firmly on the ground, it is hard work but good practice for more of the same to come. A short distance along the road a FP sign indicates the way to Sticklepath. On reaching the road (B3190) turn sharp right for a few yards then equally sharp left to Withay Farm. Ignore the sign here which points to Comberow and Tinwood and turn right down the lane into the valley and Pitt Mill which was on the outgoing route. This time however follow the road and (avoiding the sign to Leighland Chapel) keep to the path more or less south down into Broadfield Wood. Take the higher of the two paths shown on the map through the woods to Leigh Barton Farm, from here one of the many delightful RUPPS (you have been warned!) ends on the Swinhays Cross to Roadwater road with an FP sign opposite which leads to a lane and thence back into Treborough.

Walk 14

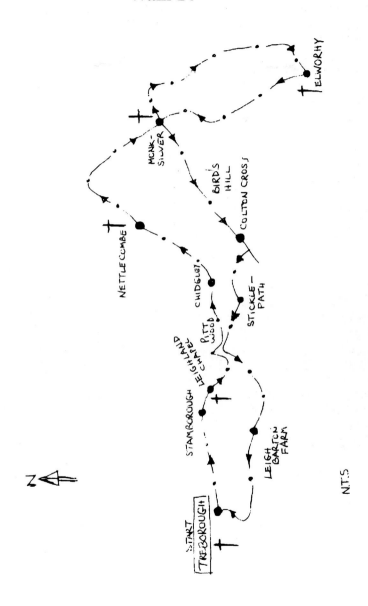

N.T.S

TREBOROUGH.
St. Peters.

The piety of people until recent times is truly remarkable.A church here could never have had a congregation of any size yet, like many others, this one has been well cared for. As recently as the first half of the century it was largely rebuilt, an idea totally out of the question today. It is suggested that it may well be the third highest church in all southern England which does seem surprising although the struggle up from Pitt Mill to Treborough tends to confirm the point. The interior is plain and simple but has that air of peace and calm typical of these moorland churches.

LEIGHLAND CHAPEL.
St. Giles.

This is the parish church apparently without a parish to go with it. Although that newfangled electric lighting has been installed the old lamps are still in place and it must be said look far more attractive (as well as warmer). Another plain but lovely old place which must once have been well attended because in the 1914/18 war twelve men served in all parts of the world and in the 1939/45 war another three did so. They might have problems finding numbers of that sort at the present time.

NETTLECOMBE.
St. Mary the Virgin.

A beautiful and well maintained church in idyllic surroundings. No doubt the close association with the Trevelyan family over the years has been the mainstay of St. Mary's and what a superb legacy it has left behind. The stone effigies of members of the Raleigh family are alone worth going a long way to see (13th century) but there is much else to intrigue the visitor. The whole environment of church and Court (once the hordes of young students at the field centre have' departed for the day) is one of peace and great historical interest.

MONKSILVER.
All Saints.

After Nettlecombe the Parish church of Monksilver might seem to be something of an anti-climax but infact is anything but. Obviously not richly endowed and relatively plain inside it is nevertheless a delightful little church, well up to the quality of Exmoor churches. The one impressive feature which stands out as one enters the place is the beautifully carved altar screen.

ELWORTHY.
St. Martin of Tours.

A most impressive name for a small country church serving a population of 82 in 1961 and 62 by 1971. The fact that it is now closed for worship but maintained by the Redundant Churches Fund is undoudtedly a fine thing because otherwise it would decay through lack of contributing population. One outstanding feature is the absolutely enormous Yew tree in the churchyard - one wonders how many bows cut from it served English archers in the Middle Ages.